Unyielding Voices: Empowering the Masses to Stand Up Against a Dictator

By Nicolas Gregg

Table of contents

Introduction:

In a world plagued by the oppressive grip of dictators, the need for change has never been more urgent. "This book" is a groundbreaking book that emboldens individuals to rise against dictators, empowering them to create a future where liberty and justice prevail. Drawing from historical lessons and modern-day struggles, this powerful guide offers invaluable insights, strategies, and inspiring stories to inspire readers to stand up, unite, and bring about lasting transformation.

Dictators have long exploited their positions of power, suppressing dissent, trampling on human rights, and stifling the voices of the oppressed. They thrive on fear, censorship, and control, leaving the masses feeling helpless and devoid of hope. But throughout history, there have been remarkable instances where ordinary people have risen against the odds, dismantling dictatorships and reclaiming their freedom.

"This book" serves as a beacon of hope, illuminating the path to liberation for those yearning for change. It delves into the stories of courageous individuals who defied oppressive regimes, offering a blueprint for resistance and inspiring readers to believe in their own capacity to make a difference. By analyzing the strategies, tactics, and principles employed by these heroes, readers can gain a deeper understanding of the dynamics of power and learn how to effectively challenge and overcome dictatorial rule.

Furthermore, "This book" explores the intersection between historical context and present-day struggles, examining how the lessons of the past can be applied to contemporary situations. It sheds light on the common tactics employed by dictators to maintain their grip on power, such as propaganda, surveillance, and the suppression of dissent. Armed with this knowledge, readers can develop a critical perspective and devise innovative ways to undermine and expose dictatorial regimes.

The book also emphasizes the importance of unity and collective action. It highlights the power of grassroots movements, social mobilization, and international solidarity in toppling dictators. By examining successful examples of resistance, readers are encouraged to build networks, forge alliances, and harness the strength of numbers to effect change.

Ultimately, "This book" aims to inspire individuals to rise against dictators and become agents of transformation in their communities. It encourages readers to embrace their inherent rights and freedoms, cultivating a sense of empowerment and the belief that change is possible. By empowering individuals with knowledge, strategies, and inspiring stories, this groundbreaking book strives to ignite a global movement for liberty, justice, and a future free from the clutches of dictatorship.

Chapter 1: Understanding the Anatomy of Dictatorship

Dictatorship is a form of government in which power is concentrated in the hands of a single individual or a small group, often achieved through force or manipulation. In this chapter, we will delve into the characteristics and tactics employed by dictators to maintain control, explore the historical context of dictatorial regimes, and examine the devastating consequences they have inflicted upon societies. Additionally, we will highlight the significance of reclaiming individual and collective freedom in the face of dictatorship.

Characteristics of Dictatorship:

Dictatorships typically exhibit certain common characteristics that distinguish them from other forms of government. These characteristics may include:

Concentration of Power:

Dictators wield an excessive amount of power, often unchecked by checks and balances or democratic institutions. They exert control over all aspects of governance, including legislation, law enforcement, the military, and the judiciary.

Suppression of Dissent:

Dictators employ various methods to suppress opposition and dissent. This can range from censorship and propaganda to surveillance, arbitrary arrests, torture, and even extrajudicial killings. By silencing dissenting voices, dictators aim to eliminate challenges to their authority.

Cult of Personality:

Dictators often cultivate a cult of personality around themselves, portraying themselves as indispensable leaders and saviors of their nations. They utilize propaganda and control over media to promote their image, fostering a sense of loyalty and adoration among their followers.

Lack of Political Pluralism:
Dictatorships are characterized by the absence of genuine political competition and pluralism. Opposition parties are often banned or marginalized, elections are manipulated or fraudulent, and the political landscape is dominated by the ruling regime.

Tactics Employed by Dictators:
Dictators employ a range of tactics to consolidate and maintain their grip on power. These tactics include:

Repression and Fear:
Dictators rely on repression and fear to control their populations. This can involve the use of secret police, surveillance, and a pervasive atmosphere of

intimidation. By instilling fear, dictators discourage dissent and maintain compliance.

 Propaganda and Manipulation:
Dictators employ propaganda and manipulation techniques to shape public opinion and control the narrative. State-controlled media and dissemination of false information serve to glorify the regime, vilify opposition, and distort reality.

Divide and Rule:
Dictators often exploit societal divisions, such as ethnic, religious, or social tensions, to maintain their power. By exacerbating these divisions, they divert attention from their oppressive policies and create a climate of conflict that reinforces their control.

 Co-optation and Patronage:
Dictators may employ patronage systems, co-opting influential individuals or groups with privileges and benefits in exchange for their loyalty. By ensuring a network of supporters, dictators reinforce their power structure and undermine potential opposition.

Historical Context and Consequences:
Throughout history, dictatorial regimes have emerged in various nations, leading to catastrophic consequences for their populations. The rise of Adolf Hitler in Nazi Germany, Joseph Stalin's Soviet Union, and more recent examples such as Saddam Hussein in Iraq and Muammar Gaddafi in Libya serve as reminders of the devastation wrought by dictators. These regimes have been responsible for mass killings, human rights abuses, economic mismanagement, and the stifling of individual freedoms.

Reclaiming Individual and Collective Freedom:
Recognizing the importance of individual and collective freedom is vital in countering and overcoming dictatorial regimes. By promoting democracy, upholding human rights, fostering transparency, and empowering civil society, individuals and communities can challenge,and obtain in collective freedom which is a significant step towards creating a society that values personal autonomy and respects the rights of its members. Individual freedom refers to the ability of

each person to make choices, express themselves, and pursue their own goals without undue interference or oppression.

Collective freedom, on the other hand, recognizes the importance of communities and society as a whole in fostering an environment where individuals can exercise their freedom. It involves the promotion of inclusive and equitable systems that protect the rights and well-being of all members, ensuring that no one is marginalized or left behind.

Reclaiming individual and collective freedom often requires challenging existing power structures, addressing systemic inequalities, and promoting social justice. It involves recognizing and confronting oppressive systems, such as discrimination based on race, gender, religion, or socioeconomic status, that limit the freedom and opportunities of certain groups of people.

Individual and collective freedom are interconnected. An environment that respects and upholds individual freedom enables people to fully participate in society and contribute to the collective well-being. At the same time, a society that values collective freedom ensures that the rights and freedoms of individuals are protected and upheld.

Reclaiming individual and collective freedom can involve various actions, such as advocating for human rights, supporting marginalized communities, promoting democratic processes, and challenging oppressive policies. It requires fostering a culture of inclusivity, tolerance, and respect for diversity.

By recognizing the importance of individual and collective freedom, we acknowledge the fundamental rights and dignity of every person. It is through the collective effort of individuals and communities that we can create a society that upholds these freedoms, promotes social justice, and fosters a sense of empowerment for all.

Chapter 2: Cultivating Resilience and Unity

Building a resilient mindset to overcome fear and intimidation

Fostering unity and solidarity among diverse communities to create a formidable force

Highlighting successful examples of grassroots movements that triumphed against oppressive rule

Section 1: Building a Resilient Mindset to Overcome Fear and Intimidation

In the face of fear and intimidation, cultivating a resilient mindset is essential for individuals and communities to overcome obstacles and thrive. Here are some strategies that can help in building such resilience:

Recognize and acknowledge fear: It is important to acknowledge and accept fear as a natural human emotion. By acknowledging fear, we can begin to understand its roots and work towards overcoming it.

Develop self-awareness: Understanding our strengths, weaknesses, and triggers can help us build resilience. Self-awareness allows us to recognize our limitations and focus on personal growth.

Practice self-care: Prioritizing self-care is crucial for building resilience. Taking care of our physical and mental well-being through activities such as exercise, meditation, and engaging in hobbies can help us better cope with challenges.

Cultivate a growth mindset: Embracing a growth mindset means viewing challenges as opportunities for learning and growth. Instead of being discouraged by setbacks, we can see them as stepping stones toward success.

Seek support: Building a support network of friends, family, or mentors can provide valuable encouragement and guidance. Sharing our fears and concerns with trusted individuals can help alleviate anxiety and provide fresh perspectives.

Set realistic goals: Breaking down larger goals into smaller, achievable tasks can make the journey less overwhelming. Celebrating small victories along the way can boost motivation and confidence.

Practice resilience-building exercises: Engaging in activities that promote resilience, such as journaling, positive affirmations, and visualization, can strengthen our ability to bounce back from adversity.

Section 2: Fostering Unity and Solidarity among Diverse Communities

Creating unity and solidarity among diverse communities is crucial in building a formidable force capable of addressing social, political, and economic challenges. Here are some ways to foster unity:

Promote dialogue and understanding: Encourage open and respectful communication among different communities. Organize events, workshops, or forums where people can share their perspectives and learn from one another.

Emphasize common goals and values: Highlight the shared goals and values that bring diverse communities together. By focusing on what unites us rather than what divides us, we can build stronger alliances.

Encourage collaboration and cooperation: Foster opportunities for collaboration between diverse communities. Encouraging joint projects, partnerships, or initiatives can promote understanding and build trust.

Address systemic inequalities: Recognize and address the systemic barriers that perpetuate inequalities among different communities. Advocate for policies and reforms that promote equity and social justice.

Celebrate diversity: Embrace and celebrate the diversity within and among communities. Create spaces where different cultures, traditions, and identities are respected and valued.

Engage in collective action: Encourage collective action to address common concerns and challenges. By organizing protests, rallies, or campaigns, diverse communities can amplify their voices and effect change.

Educate and raise awareness: Promote education and awareness about different cultures, histories, and experiences. Foster an environment that values diversity and rejects discrimination.

Section 3: Highlighting Successful Examples of Grassroots Movements

Grassroots movements have played a significant role throughout history in driving social, political, and environmental change. Here are some successful examples of grassroots movements that have made a lasting impact:

Civil Rights Movement (United States, 1950s-1960s): The Civil Rights Movement aimed to secure equal rights and end racial segregation and discrimination against African Americans. Led by influential figures such as Martin Luther King Jr., Rosa Parks, and Malcolm X, this movement employed peaceful protests, sit-ins, and marches to bring attention to racial inequality. It eventually led to landmark legislation, including the Civil Rights Act of 1964 and the Voting Rights Act of 1965.

Solidarity Movement (Poland, 1980-1989): The Solidarity Movement emerged as a response to the oppressive communist regime in Poland. Led by Lech Walesa, this trade union movement organized strikes, protests, and demonstrations to demand workers' rights, freedom of speech, and political reforms. It eventually led to the fall of communism in Poland and inspired similar movements across Eastern Europe.

Anti-Apartheid Movement (South Africa and globally, 1950s-1990s): The Anti-Apartheid Movement aimed to end the institutionalized racial segregation and discrimination in South Africa. Through boycotts, divestment campaigns, and international pressure, this movement garnered widespread support and raised awareness about the injustices of apartheid. It played a crucial role in isolating the apartheid regime, leading to the release of Nelson Mandela and the eventual dismantling of apartheid.

Women's Suffrage Movement (Global, late 19th century-early 20th century): The women's suffrage movement fought for women's right to vote and gender equality. Activists like Susan B. Anthony, Elizabeth Cady Stanton, and Emmeline Pankhurst organized marches, protests, and lobbying efforts to advocate for women's suffrage. Their tireless activism led to significant achievements, such as the passage of the 19th Amendment in the United States and the enfranchisement of women in many other countries.

Environmental Movement (Global, ongoing): The environmental movement encompasses a range of grassroots efforts focused on addressing environmental issues and promoting sustainability. Groups like

Greenpeace, 350.org, and Fridays for Future have mobilized millions of people worldwide through protests, grassroots organizing, and advocacy. These movements have raised awareness about climate change, pushed for renewable energy sources, and influenced policy decisions to protect the environment.

Marriage Equality Movement (Global, ongoing): The marriage equality movement advocates for equal rights for LGBTQ+ individuals, specifically the right to marry and have their unions recognized legally. Through grassroots organizing, legal challenges, and public campaigns, this movement has achieved significant milestones, including the legalization of same-sex marriage in numerous countries and the United States.

These examples highlight the power of grassroots movements in shaping societal change. By mobilizing communities, raising awareness, and advocating for justice, grassroots movements have the potential to create lasting impact and inspire future generations.

Chapter 3: Harnessing the Power of Information and Communication

Exploiting the potential of technology and social media to organize and mobilize the masses:

In today's digital age, technology and social media have become powerful tools for organizing and mobilizing people on a massive scale. The widespread accessibility of the internet and the prevalence of social networking platforms offer unprecedented opportunities for individuals and communities to connect, collaborate, and effect change. To harness the potential of technology and social media, several strategies can be employed:

Building online communities: Creating online platforms and communities centered around specific causes or interests can help like-minded individuals come together, share information, and organize collective action. These communities can serve as hubs for exchanging ideas, coordinating efforts, and mobilizing resources.

Crowdsourcing and crowdfunding: Technology allows for the rapid dissemination of information and the aggregation of resources. Crowdsourcing can be used to gather information, generate ideas, and solve problems collectively. Crowdfunding platforms can help raise funds for projects and initiatives, enabling individuals and organizations to achieve their goals.

Leveraging social media platforms: Social media platforms provide a wide reach and allow for the rapid dissemination of information. Utilizing social media effectively involves creating engaging content, using hashtags and trending topics, and fostering dialogue to generate momentum and build support for causes or events.

Strategies for circumventing censorship and spreading awareness globally:

In some parts of the world, governments or other entities may impose censorship on information flow to control narratives and limit public awareness. Overcoming censorship and spreading awareness globally require innovative approaches:

Virtual Private Networks (VPNs) and proxy servers: VPNs and proxy servers can help individuals bypass government censorship by encrypting their internet traffic and routing it through servers located in countries with more lenient online regulations. This allows people to access blocked websites and communicate securely.

Secure communication tools: Encrypted messaging apps and tools offer a secure means of communication, protecting conversations from surveillance or interception. Examples include Signal, Telegram, or even encrypted email services.

Peer-to-peer networks and decentralized platforms: Utilizing peer-to-peer networks and decentralized platforms ensures that information is distributed across a network of users rather than being stored in a central server. This approach makes it more difficult for authorities to censor or shut down information dissemination.

Nurturing a culture of critical thinking and media literacy to combat propaganda:

In an era of information overload and the spread of misinformation, fostering critical thinking and media literacy is crucial. Individuals need to develop the skills to critically analyze and evaluate the information they consume. Strategies for nurturing a culture of critical thinking and media literacy include:

Education and awareness programs: Incorporate media literacy education into school curricula and develop public awareness campaigns to promote critical thinking skills. These initiatives should focus on teaching individuals how to evaluate sources, fact-check information, and identify bias or propaganda.

Fact-checking organizations: Support and promote independent fact-checking organizations that help verify the accuracy of news and information. Encourage individuals to consult these organizations before accepting information at face value.

Encourage diverse perspectives: Foster an environment where individuals are exposed to a range of viewpoints and encourage respectful dialogue and debate. This helps develop critical thinking skills and reduces susceptibility to propaganda.

Media literacy in digital platforms: Collaborate with social media companies to integrate media literacy features within their platforms. This can include tools to flag false information, provide context, and encourage users to think critically about the content they encounter.

By exploiting technology, circumventing censorship, and promoting critical thinking and media literacy, individuals and communities can harness the power of information and communication to organize, mobilize, and combat propaganda effectively

Exploiting the potential of technology and social media to organize and mobilize the masses:

Exploiting the potential of technology and social media to organize and mobilize the masses can be a powerful tool for social and political change. Here are some key points to consider when utilizing technology and social media for organizing and mobilizing:

Utilize social media platforms: Platforms like Facebook, Twitter, Instagram, and YouTube offer vast networks and reach. Create dedicated pages, groups, or channels to share information, updates, and calls to action. Engage with your audience through regular posts, videos, and live streams.

Develop a clear message: Craft a compelling message that resonates with your target audience. Clearly articulate your goals, values, and the change you seek to bring about. Make sure your message is concise, impactful, and shareable across different social media platforms.

Build an online community: Foster a sense of community among your followers. Encourage them to share their stories, ideas, and experiences related to the cause. Engage in conversations, respond to comments, and facilitate discussions to build a strong online support network.

Create shareable content: Develop visually appealing and shareable content such as infographics, videos, memes, and blog posts. These can help convey your message in an easily digestible format and increase the likelihood of your content being shared across social media platforms.

Leverage influencers and partnerships: Collaborate with influencers, activists, and organizations that align with your cause. Partnering with individuals or groups who have a large following can amplify your message and extend your reach to a wider audience.

Organize online events: Plan and host online events such as webinars, virtual conferences, and live streams to engage your audience and provide them with valuable information. These events can also serve as platforms for networking, sharing experiences, and organizing collective actions.

Use hashtags strategically: Identify relevant hashtags that are popular and widely used within your target audience. Incorporate these hashtags into your social media posts to increase visibility and make it easier for people to find and join conversations related to your cause.

Call for action: Clearly outline actionable steps that individuals can take to support your cause. This can include signing petitions, contacting legislators, attending rallies or protests, volunteering, or donating to related organizations. Provide easy-to-follow instructions and share resources to empower your followers to take meaningful action.

Monitor and analyze data: Use social media analytics tools to track engagement, reach, and the effectiveness of your campaigns. Analyzing data can help you understand what strategies are working and where you may need to make adjustments to maximize impact.

Prioritize privacy and security: When organizing and mobilizing online, it's important to prioritize privacy and security. Educate your followers about potential risks and encourage them to protect their personal information. Use secure communication channels and take necessary precautions to ensure the safety of your online community.

Remember that while technology and social media offer great potential, building real-world connections and engaging in offline actions are also crucial for creating lasting change. Balance your online efforts with on-the-ground organizing and mobilization to achieve the greatest impact.

Highlighting the risks and challenges associated with the use of technology in resistance movement

While technology has undoubtedly revolutionized the way we communicate, gather information, and organize ourselves, it also carries risks and challenges, especially when used in resistance movements. Here are some key aspects highlighting the dark side of technology in this context:

Surveillance and Monitoring: Technology enables governments and other powerful entities to monitor and surveil individuals and resistance movements more effectively. Digital communications, social media activities, and even location data can be tracked, compromising the privacy and security of activists. Governments can employ sophisticated surveillance tools, such as facial recognition, data mining, and network analysis, to identify and target individuals involved in resistance movements.

Cyber Attacks and Hacking: As technology advances, so do the methods used to exploit it. Resistance movements heavily relying on technology are vulnerable to cyber attacks and hacking attempts. Governments or other adversaries may employ tactics like distributed denial-of-service (DDoS) attacks, malware, phishing, or social engineering to compromise activists' systems, steal sensitive information, or disrupt their operations.

Infiltration and Co-optation: Technology platforms, including social media and messaging apps, can be infiltrated by adversaries seeking to identify and undermine resistance movements. Fake accounts, trolls, or individuals with ulterior motives may join online communities, spreading misinformation, sowing discord, or even gathering intelligence to undermine the movement's goals.

Disinformation and Manipulation: Technology has facilitated the rapid dissemination of information, but it has also given rise to the spread of disinformation and propaganda. Adversaries can exploit social media algorithms and echo chambers to manipulate public opinion, discredit resistance movements, or create confusion among their members. Deepfakes and other forms of manipulated media can further complicate efforts to discern truth from falsehood.

Dependency and Infrastructure Risks: Relying heavily on technology for communication, coordination, and information sharing can make resistance movements vulnerable to disruptions. Governments may intentionally disrupt internet access, block specific websites or apps, or employ other forms of digital censorship to suppress dissent. Additionally, the reliance on digital infrastructure creates a dependency that can be exploited by adversaries through infrastructure attacks, cutting off crucial communication channels.

Ethical Dilemmas: The use of technology in resistance movements can also raise ethical dilemmas. For instance, activists might grapple with balancing the need for secure communication against the potential risk of technology providers sharing their data with governments. The use of encryption and anonymization tools, which can be essential for security, may also invite scrutiny and suspicion from authorities.

To address these risks and challenges, resistance movements must be vigilant and proactive in adopting countermeasures. This includes implementing robust security practices, using encrypted communication channels, conducting regular digital hygiene practices, educating members about the risks, and staying informed about emerging threats. Collaboration with experts in digital security and privacy can also help mitigate the dark side of technology in resistance movements.

Chapter 4: Nonviolent Resistance: The Path to Change

Nonviolent resistance, also known as nonviolent action or civil resistance, is a powerful method of bringing about social and political change without the use of violence. This chapter will explore the principles and effectiveness of nonviolent resistance movements, focusing on tactical approaches such as civil disobedience, strikes, and boycotts. It will also examine case studies of iconic figures and movements that successfully toppled dictators and oppressive regimes through nonviolent means.

Principles of Nonviolent Resistance:
Nonviolent resistance is grounded in a set of principles that guide its strategies and actions. Some key principles include:

a. Nonviolence: Nonviolent resistance rejects the use of physical force, instead emphasizing peaceful methods to challenge injustice and oppression.

b. Active Nonviolence: Nonviolent action requires active engagement and participation, rather than passive acceptance of the status quo.

c. Moral High Ground: Nonviolent resistance seeks to maintain a moral high ground, presenting a stark contrast to the oppressive regime's tactics and actions.

d. Unity and Solidarity: Successful nonviolent movements often emphasize unity and solidarity among diverse groups, transcending divisions and building broad-based coalitions.

e. Persistence: Nonviolent resistance requires patience and persistence, as change often takes time and sustained effort.

Tactical Approaches in Nonviolent Resistance:

Nonviolent resistance employs various tactical approaches to challenge oppressive systems and bring about change. Some common tactics include:

a. Civil Disobedience: Civil disobedience involves intentionally violating unjust laws or regulations as a form of protest. This tactic aims to expose the injustice of the laws and provoke a response from authorities.

b. Strikes and Boycotts: Strikes involve organized work stoppages to disrupt economic activity and put pressure on authorities. Boycotts, on the other hand, involve refusing to participate in certain activities or purchase certain products as a means of economic leverage.

c. Demonstrations and Protests: Peaceful demonstrations and protests are a central feature of nonviolent resistance. They can include marches, sit-ins, rallies, and other forms of public expression to raise awareness and garner support.

d. Civil Disruption: Nonviolent movements may engage in acts of civil disruption, such as sit-ins, blockades, or occupations, to disrupt the functioning of oppressive systems and draw attention to their cause.

Case Studies of Iconic Figures and Movements:

a. Mahatma Gandhi and the Indian Independence Movement: Mahatma Gandhi led a nonviolent resistance movement against British colonial rule in India. Through civil disobedience, strikes, and boycotts, Gandhi and his followers achieved independence for India in 1947.

b. Martin Luther King Jr. and the Civil Rights Movement: Martin Luther King Jr. advocated for racial equality and civil rights in the United States. Through nonviolent protests, such as the Montgomery Bus Boycott and the March on Washington, the Civil Rights Movement successfully dismantled segregation and advanced civil rights legislation.

c. Nelson Mandela and the Anti-Apartheid Movement: Nelson Mandela played a pivotal role in the nonviolent struggle against apartheid in South Africa. Through boycotts, strikes, and civil disobedience, the movement achieved the end of apartheid and the establishment of a democratic South Africa.

d. The People Power Revolution in the Philippines: In 1986, a nonviolent uprising known as the People Power Revolution ousted dictator Ferdinand Marcos in the Philippines. The movement utilized various tactics, including mass protests and civil disobedience, to peacefully reclaim democracy.

Nonviolent resistance has proven to be a potent and transformative force throughout history. By adhering to principles of nonviolence and employing tactical approaches such as civil disobedience, strikes, and boycotts, individuals and movements have successfully challenged oppressive regimes and brought about significant social and political change.

Chapter 5: Building International Support

In order to effectively address global challenges and advance national interests, it is crucial for nations to build international support. This chapter explores strategies to garner support from the international community and organizations, advocate for diplomatic pressure, economic sanctions, and humanitarian intervention, and utilize strategic alliances and partnerships to amplify the message and garner resources.

Engaging the International Community and Organizations:

To build international support, it is essential to engage with various stakeholders, including other nations, international organizations, and non-governmental organizations. Here are some strategies to consider:

a. Diplomatic Outreach: Actively engage in diplomatic efforts to promote dialogue, understanding, and cooperation. This involves establishing and maintaining diplomatic relations with key countries and actively participating in international forums such as the United Nations, regional organizations, and multilateral summits.

b. Public Diplomacy: Utilize public diplomacy techniques to promote the nation's values, culture, and policies to the international community. This can include cultural exchanges, educational programs, international media engagement, and hosting international events.

c. Humanitarian Assistance: Provide humanitarian aid and support to countries in need, especially during times of crisis or natural disasters. This demonstrates the nation's commitment to global welfare and can help build goodwill and support.

Advocating for Diplomatic Pressure, Economic Sanctions, and Humanitarian Intervention:

In certain situations, advocating for diplomatic pressure, economic sanctions, or humanitarian intervention may be necessary to address global challenges or promote national interests. Here's how these approaches can be utilized effectively:

a. Diplomatic Pressure: Engage in diplomatic negotiations and dialogue to resolve conflicts, promote peace, and address concerns. This can involve coordinating with like-minded countries to exert diplomatic pressure on parties involved in disputes, using diplomatic channels to voice concerns, and pursuing peaceful resolutions through mediation or negotiation.

b. Economic Sanctions: Advocate for targeted economic sanctions to pressure countries or entities engaged in activities detrimental to international peace, security, or human rights. Collaborate with international partners to enforce these sanctions effectively, ensuring they are carefully designed to minimize unintended negative consequences.

c. Humanitarian Intervention: In extreme cases where populations are subjected to gross human rights abuses or facing severe humanitarian crises, advocate for humanitarian intervention. This may involve mobilizing international coalitions, coordinating with relevant international organizations, and taking necessary actions to protect vulnerable populations.

Utilizing Strategic Alliances and Partnerships:
Strategic alliances and partnerships with other nations, regional organizations, and international institutions can greatly amplify the message, garner support, and access additional resources. Here's how to leverage these alliances effectively:
a. Forming Coalitions: Identify common interests and concerns with other nations or regional organizations and form coalitions to collectively address challenges. These coalitions can amplify the nation's voice on the international stage and increase the likelihood of success.

b. Leveraging International Institutions: Engage with international organizations such as the United Nations,

World Trade Organization, World Health Organization, and regional organizations to leverage their resources, expertise, and networks. Active participation in these institutions allows the nation to shape policies, influence decisions, and build partnerships.

c. Promoting Shared Interests: Identify areas of shared interests with other countries and collaborate on initiatives that align with those interests. This can include joint research projects, technology sharing, economic partnerships, and security cooperation, fostering mutually beneficial relationships.

Conclusion:
Building international support is crucial for addressing global challenges and advancing national interests. By engaging the international community and organizations, advocating for diplomatic pressure, economic sanctions, and humanitarian intervention when necessary, and utilizing strategic alliances and partnerships, nations can strengthen their position,

amplify their message, and effectively address global issues while promoting their own interests.

Chapter 6: The Role of Leadership and Empowering Future Generations

In the journey towards progress and social change, effective leadership plays a crucial role in guiding movements towards success. This chapter focuses on the importance of nurturing leadership qualities and empowering future generations to become agents of change. It also addresses the challenges associated with transitioning from dictatorship to democracy and the significance of fostering inclusive governance.

Nurturing Effective Leadership:
Effective leadership is essential for mobilizing and inspiring individuals to work towards a common goal. To nurture effective leadership, it is important to focus on the following aspects:

a) Vision and Purpose: Leaders need to articulate a compelling vision and purpose that resonates with the aspirations of the people. This vision should provide a clear direction and inspire collective action.

b) Communication and Empathy: Leaders should possess strong communication skills and the ability to empathize with the concerns and needs of the people. Effective communication helps in building trust, fostering collaboration, and motivating others to take action.

c) Integrity and Ethical Conduct: Leaders must exhibit integrity and ethical conduct, serving as role models for others. Transparency, honesty, and accountability are vital in gaining the trust and respect of the community.

d) Continuous Learning and Adaptability: Leaders should be open to learning, self-improvement, and adapting to changing circumstances. They must be willing to listen to diverse perspectives and be open to new ideas and innovative approaches.

Encouraging Youth Participation:

Empowering future generations and encouraging their active participation in social and political processes is critical for sustainable development. The following strategies can help in engaging youth and empowering them to be agents of change:

a) Education and Skill Development: Providing quality education and skill development opportunities equips youth with the necessary knowledge and tools to actively participate in society. It enhances their critical thinking, problem-solving abilities, and leadership skills.

b) Mentorship and Guidance: Establishing mentorship programs where experienced leaders guide and support young individuals can accelerate their personal and professional growth. Mentorship fosters the transfer of knowledge, builds confidence, and encourages youth to take on leadership roles.

c) Youth Representation and Participation: Actively involving youth in decision-making processes at various levels, such as local, national, and international, ensures their voices are heard and considered. Creating platforms for youth-led initiatives and organizations promotes their active participation and empowers them to contribute to positive change.

Addressing the Challenges of Transitioning from Dictatorship to Democracy:
Transitioning from a dictatorship to a democracy poses significant challenges. It requires a deliberate effort to establish inclusive governance structures and processes. Key considerations include:

a) Truth and Reconciliation: Addressing past human rights abuses, promoting healing, and fostering reconciliation are fundamental steps in building a democratic society. Establishing truth commissions, supporting transitional justice mechanisms, and providing reparations can help address historical grievances.

b) Democratic Institutions and Rule of Law: Strengthening democratic institutions, such as independent judiciaries, free media, and robust civil society organizations, is crucial for upholding the rule of law. These institutions serve as checks and balances, ensuring accountability and transparency in governance.

c) Citizen Engagement and Participation: Encouraging citizen engagement in democratic processes through civic education, voter registration campaigns, and open dialogue platforms helps build an informed and active citizenry. It ensures the inclusion of diverse perspectives and enhances the legitimacy of democratic governance.

Fostering Inclusive Governance:
Inclusive governance involves creating structures and processes that enable the participation of all individuals, irrespective of their background, in decision-making and policy formulation. The following steps can foster inclusive governance:

a) Diversity and Representation: Ensuring diverse representation in decision-making bodies, including gender, ethnicity, age, and socio-economic background, enhances the inclusivity and effectiveness of governance. Affirmative action

Chapter 7: Beyond the Dictatorship

Transitioning from a dictatorship to a democratic system is a complex process that requires careful planning and implementation. This chapter will delve into the challenges and opportunities that arise during the post-dictatorship phase, offering insights and recommendations for a successful transition.

Building democratic institutions:

Establishing a constitution: Creating a new constitution or amending the existing one to ensure the protection of human rights, separation of powers, and checks and balances.

Electoral reforms: Implementing fair and transparent electoral processes, including voter registration, campaign financing regulations, and electoral oversight mechanisms.

Strengthening the judiciary: Ensuring an independent judiciary that upholds the rule of law, safeguards individual rights, and holds perpetrators accountable for past human rights abuses.

Fostering a culture of democratic participation:

Civic education: Promoting civic education programs to empower citizens with the knowledge and skills necessary to actively participate in the democratic process.

Political party development: Encouraging the formation of diverse political parties and facilitating their participation in the political arena to promote a pluralistic and inclusive democracy.

Engaging civil society: Creating an enabling environment for civil society organizations to operate freely, advocate for citizens' rights, and contribute to democratic governance.

Reconciliation and justice: Addressing the need for truth, justice, and accountability to heal the wounds inflicted by a dictatorial regime.

Transitioning from a dictatorship requires addressing the legacy of human rights abuses and promoting reconciliation among the affected population. This section focuses on the crucial elements of truth, justice, and accountability to facilitate healing and promote a more inclusive society.

Truth and reconciliation commissions:

Establishing a truth commission: Creating an independent body to investigate and document past human rights violations, provide a platform for victims to share their experiences, and foster national healing.
Promoting transparency: Ensuring the commission's proceedings are transparent, inclusive, and accessible to the public to restore trust in the process and build a shared understanding of the past.
Transitional justice mechanisms:

Prosecution of perpetrators: Holding those responsible for human rights abuses accountable through fair trials, ensuring that justice is served and providing closure for victims.
Reparations for victims: Implementing reparations programs to compensate victims, restore their dignity,

and address the material and psychological harm they have suffered.

Institutional reforms: Transforming security forces, justice systems, and public administration to prevent future human rights violations and promote accountability.

Safeguarding democracy: Outlining steps to protect and strengthen democratic institutions to prevent future dictatorships.

To prevent the recurrence of dictatorship, it is essential to safeguard democratic institutions and foster a resilient democratic culture. This section explores strategies to strengthen democracy and protect it from potential threats.

Institutional checks and balances:

Separation of powers: Ensuring an independent judiciary, a functioning legislature, and an executive branch that respects and abides by democratic norms and principles.

Constitutional safeguards: Incorporating mechanisms in the constitution that prevent the concentration of power, such as term limits, decentralization, and protection of minority rights.

Civic engagement and participation:

Protecting civil liberties: Safeguarding freedom of expression, assembly, and association, which are fundamental pillars of a healthy democracy.

Encouraging citizen participation: Promoting mechanisms for citizen engagement, such as public consultations, citizen assemblies, and participatory budgeting, to foster a sense of ownership and accountability.

International support and cooperation:

Diplomatic pressure: Garnering international support and pressure to uphold democratic values and hold governments accountable for any authoritarian tendencies.

Assistance and capacity-building

Here are additional points to consider in each section:

Strengthening the civil service: Reforming the bureaucracy to ensure professionalism, transparency, and meritocracy in public administration.

Promoting decentralization: Empowering local governments and fostering participatory decision-making at the grassroots level.

Media freedom and independence: Ensuring a free and independent media that can act as a watchdog and provide diverse and unbiased information to the public.

Fostering a culture of democratic participation:

Youth engagement: Encouraging the active participation of young people in political processes and decision-making, as they are the future of democracy.

Encouraging women's participation: Promoting gender equality in politics and ensuring the inclusion of women in leadership positions.

Reconciliation and justice:

Truth and reconciliation commissions:

Public awareness and education: Conducting outreach campaigns to raise awareness about the commission's work and promote public participation.
Witness protection and support: Establishing mechanisms to protect witnesses and provide them with necessary support throughout the process.
Transitional justice mechanisms:

International cooperation: Seeking international support for the prosecution of perpetrators, including extradition and sharing of information and expertise.
Combating impunity: Strengthening the judiciary's capacity to handle complex cases and ensuring that no one is above the law.
Safeguarding democracy:

Institutional checks and balances:

Independent election commissions: Establishing independent bodies to oversee elections and ensure their fairness and integrity.

Anti-corruption measures: Implementing robust anti-corruption mechanisms and promoting transparency and accountability in public administration.

Civic engagement and participation:

Strengthening civil society organizations: Providing resources and support to civil society organizations that promote democratic values and engage in advocacy and monitoring.

Digital democracy: Embracing technology to enhance citizen participation, such as e-governance platforms and online consultation tools.

International support and cooperation:

Democracy promotion programs: Engaging in international initiatives and programs that support democratic governance, including technical assistance and capacity-building for democratic institutions.

Peer learning and knowledge sharing: Establishing networks and platforms for countries transitioning to democracy to share experiences and best practices.

These additional points provide a more comprehensive framework for exploring the challenges and opportunities in transitioning to democracy, fostering reconciliation and justice, and safeguarding democratic institutions.

Chapter 8 : Modern day democracy

Democracy is a system of government in which power is vested in the people, who exercise it directly or through elected representatives. It is derived from the Greek words "demos," meaning "people," and "kratos," meaning "rule" or "power." In a democratic system, the citizens have the right to participate in decision-making processes, either by voting directly on issues or by electing representatives to make decisions on their behalf.

Key features of democracy include political freedom, equality, and the protection of individual rights. Democracy typically involves regular free and fair elections, where citizens can choose their leaders and representatives. It also encompasses the protection of civil liberties, such as freedom of speech, assembly, and the press, as well as the rule of law, which ensures that laws apply equally to all individuals.

Democracy promotes the idea that all individuals should have an equal voice and influence in shaping the policies and laws that govern them. It recognizes the inherent dignity and worth of every person and aims to create a system that allows for peaceful and orderly decision-making processes.

There are different forms of democracy, including direct democracy, representative democracy, and various hybrid models. In direct democracy, citizens directly participate in decision-making through referendums or initiatives. Representative democracy, which is more common, involves citizens electing representatives who make decisions on their behalf. Hybrid models combine elements of both direct and representative democracy.

While democracy is generally seen as a desirable form of government, it is important to note that it can take various forms and face challenges. These challenges may include ensuring equal participation and representation, preventing the concentration of power, combating corruption, and protecting minority rights. Nonetheless, democracy remains a widely embraced system of governance that seeks to balance the interests and rights of individuals with the needs and aspirations of society as a whole.

Principles of Democracy: Democracy is based on several key principles, including popular sovereignty (the power rests with the people), political equality (every citizen has equal rights and opportunities to participate), majority rule with minority rights (decisions are made by the majority, but minority rights are protected), and the rule of law (everyone is subject to the same laws).

Fundamental Rights and Freedoms: Democracy emphasizes the protection of fundamental rights and freedoms. These may include freedom of speech, press, assembly, and religion, as well as the right to a fair trial, privacy, and equal protection under the law. These rights are considered essential for the functioning of a democratic society and the development of individuals.

Separation of Powers: Democracy often incorporates a system of checks and balances through the separation of powers. Typically, there are three branches of government: the legislative, executive, and judicial branches. Each branch has specific roles and responsibilities to prevent the concentration of power and ensure accountability.

Civil Society and Civic Engagement: Democracy thrives when there is an active civil society and robust civic engagement. Civil society refers to organizations and groups that operate independently from the government, such as NGOs, trade unions, and community organizations. Civic engagement involves citizens actively participating in public affairs, including voting, attending public meetings, and engaging in peaceful protests.

Pluralism and Diversity: Democracy recognizes and respects the diversity of society, including different opinions, beliefs, and identities. It allows for peaceful coexistence and the accommodation of various interests and perspectives. Pluralism encourages dialogue, negotiation, and compromise to reach inclusive and fair decisions.

Peaceful Transition of Power: In a democratic system, power is typically transferred peacefully through elections or other established mechanisms. This allows for stability, predictability, and the peaceful resolution of conflicts. It also provides opportunities for new leaders and ideas to emerge.

Democratic Challenges: While democracy has many advantages, it also faces challenges. These may include voter apathy, political polarization, the influence of money in politics, the rise of populism, threats to freedom of the press, and the manipulation of information and disinformation. These challenges require ongoing efforts to strengthen and protect democratic institutions.

It's important to note that democracy is a broad and evolving concept, and its implementation can vary across different countries and contexts. The specific features and practices of democracy may differ, but the underlying goal is to ensure government of the people, by the people, and for the people.

Benefits of modern day democracy
Democracy offers several benefits that contribute to the well-being and development of societies. Here are some key benefits of democracy:

Political Stability: Democracy provides a framework for peaceful and stable governance. Through regular elections and the peaceful transition of power, it helps to prevent political upheaval, coups, and violent conflicts that can arise in autocratic or authoritarian regimes. The stability offered by democracy creates an environment conducive to economic growth, social progress, and the protection of individual rights.

Protection of Individual Rights: Democracy places a strong emphasis on the protection of individual rights and freedoms. It recognizes the inherent dignity and worth of every person and strives to ensure their fundamental rights, such as freedom of speech, assembly, and religion, as well as the right to a fair trial, privacy, and equal treatment under the law. Democratic systems typically have independent judiciaries that safeguard these rights and provide a mechanism for seeking justice.

Popular Participation and Representation: Democracy allows citizens to participate in decision-making processes and have a say in the policies that affect their lives. Through voting, citizens can choose their leaders, express their preferences, and hold them accountable for their actions. Elected representatives act as a voice for the people and work towards the collective interests of the society. This participatory aspect of democracy helps to ensure that policies are responsive to the needs and aspirations of the people.

Social and Economic Development: Democracy has been associated with higher levels of social and economic development. It fosters an environment that encourages innovation, entrepreneurship, and investment. By providing political stability, protecting property rights, and promoting the rule of law, democracy creates conditions for economic growth and prosperity. Additionally, democratic governments tend to prioritize education, healthcare, infrastructure, and social welfare, which contribute to overall societal development.

Peaceful Conflict Resolution: Democratic systems offer mechanisms for peaceful conflict resolution and negotiation. Through dialogue, negotiation, and compromise, diverse interests and opinions can be accommodated within the democratic framework. This helps to prevent violent conflicts and allows for the peaceful resolution of disputes, ensuring social harmony and stability.

Accountability and Transparency: Democracy promotes accountability and transparency in governance. Elected representatives are accountable to the people who can hold them responsible for their actions through elections and other mechanisms. Democratic systems often have checks and balances, independent media, and oversight institutions that help prevent corruption and abuse of power. Transparency in decision-making processes and access to information enable citizens to make informed choices and hold their governments accountable.

These benefits highlight how democracy can contribute to the overall well-being, prosperity, and progress of societies. However, it's important to note that the effectiveness of democracy in delivering these benefits can vary depending on various factors such as the strength of democratic institutions, political culture, socioeconomic conditions, and historical context.

The shortcomings of modern day democracy:

While democracy offers significant benefits, it also faces several shortcomings and challenges in modern times. Here are some of the key shortcomings of modern-day democracy:

Voter Apathy and Disengagement: One of the major challenges is voter apathy and disengagement. Many citizens are disillusioned with politics, leading to low voter turnout and decreased participation in democratic processes. This can undermine the legitimacy and representation of elected officials and weaken the democratic system.

Political Polarization: Modern democracies often experience increased political polarization, where opposing political groups become deeply divided and entrenched in their positions. This can hinder effective governance, compromise, and the ability to address pressing issues. Polarization may also lead to a lack of cooperation and gridlock in decision-making processes.

Influence of Money in Politics: The influence of money in politics can undermine the democratic process. Wealthy individuals, corporations, and interest groups often have significant resources to shape public opinion, fund campaigns, and exert undue influence on policy decisions. This can result in unequal representation and limited access to power for those without financial resources.

Rise of Populism: Populism, characterized by the appeal to the interests and emotions of the general population, has gained prominence in many democratic societies. Populist leaders often exploit public dissatisfaction with the political establishment, promoting simplistic solutions, and engaging in divisive rhetoric. This can undermine democratic institutions, erode democratic norms, and lead to policies that may not be in the long-term interest of the society.

Disinformation and Manipulation: The spread of disinformation and manipulation of information through social media and other channels pose significant challenges to modern democracies. False or misleading information can influence public opinion, distort facts, and undermine trust in democratic institutions. This can lead to uninformed decision-making and polarized societies.

Minority Rights and Inclusivity: While democracy aims to protect minority rights, there can be challenges in ensuring their full inclusion and representation. Minority groups, whether based on ethnicity, religion, gender, or other factors, may face discrimination, marginalization, or limited access to political power. This can result in underrepresentation and the neglect of their specific needs and concerns.

Short-Term Focus and Policy Gridlock: Democracies sometimes struggle with short-term thinking and policy gridlock. Elected officials may prioritize short-term goals to secure re-election, which can hinder long-term planning and solutions to complex issues. Additionally, the need for consensus-building and compromise can sometimes lead to policy gridlock, especially when political parties or factions have opposing interests and are unwilling to find common ground.

It's important to note that these shortcomings do not imply the failure of democracy as a system of governance, but rather highlight areas that require attention and reform to strengthen democratic institutions and ensure their effectiveness. Democracies need ongoing efforts to address these challenges and uphold the principles of accountability, transparency, inclusivity, and civic engagement.

The various ways and strategies to strengthen democracy

To strengthen democracy, various strategies and measures can be implemented. Here are some key ways to enhance and reinforce democratic systems:

Promote Civic Education: Providing robust civic education is crucial to foster an informed and engaged citizenry. Education systems should emphasize democratic values, institutions, and processes, teaching students about their rights, responsibilities, and the importance of active participation in democratic decision-making.

Ensure Free and Fair Elections: Ensuring the integrity and credibility of elections is essential. Electoral systems should be transparent, inclusive, and designed to prevent fraud and manipulation. Measures such as voter registration reforms, independent election commissions, and transparent campaign financing regulations can help maintain trust in the electoral process.

Enhance Political Participation and Engagement: Encouraging and facilitating citizen participation is vital for a healthy democracy. Efforts can include initiatives such as town hall meetings, public consultations, and platforms for citizen feedback. Embracing digital technologies and e-democracy tools can also provide broader avenues for engagement and participation.

Strengthen Democratic Institutions: Strong and independent institutions are the backbone of a robust democracy. This includes a well-functioning judiciary, impartial election commissions, effective legislative bodies, and transparent and accountable executive branches. Building and maintaining the capacity, independence, and integrity of these institutions are essential for upholding the rule of law and protecting democratic principles.

Safeguard Freedom of Expression and Media: Freedom of expression and a free press are critical pillars of democracy. Governments should protect the rights of individuals and journalists to express their opinions, investigate issues, and hold those in power accountable. Ensuring media plurality, promoting media literacy, and combating disinformation are also essential in preserving the credibility and effectiveness of democratic discourse.

Foster a Culture of Dialogue and Compromise: Nurturing a culture of dialogue, respect, and compromise among political actors is crucial for effective governance. Encouraging cross-party collaboration, promoting bipartisan approaches, and fostering inclusive decision-making processes can help overcome polarization and promote constructive debate.

Combat Corruption and Ensure Accountability: Corruption undermines democratic systems and erodes public trust. Governments should implement strong anti-corruption measures, enforce ethical standards, and promote transparency and accountability in public administration. Independent anti-corruption bodies and mechanisms for reporting and investigating corruption allegations are vital in maintaining the integrity of democratic institutions.

Promote Inclusivity and Protect Minority Rights: Democracies must strive to ensure the full inclusion and representation of all segments of society. Steps should be taken to promote equal opportunities, protect the rights of marginalized groups, and address systemic discrimination. Affirmative action policies and inclusive decision-making processes can help ensure diverse voices are heard and taken into account.

Encourage International Cooperation: International cooperation and collaboration play a crucial role in strengthening democracy globally. Governments, civil society organizations, and international institutions should work together to promote democratic values, share best practices, and support democratic transitions in countries where democracy is fragile or emerging.

It's important to note that strengthening democracy is an ongoing process that requires sustained commitment, engagement from citizens, and adaptability to changing circumstances. The strategies and measures mentioned above can serve as a foundation for promoting and enhancing democratic systems, but they should be tailored to the specific context and needs of each country.